Tracti

& Recollections

Aveling & Porter of Rochester

Contents

Frontispiece: The 'dancing horse' emblem and the motto 'Invicta' carried by Aveling & Porter engines is also the emblem of the county of Kent.

First published in 2011
British Library Cataloguing in Publication Data
A catalogue record for this book is available from the British Library.
ISBN 978 1 85794 379 5

Introduction

Aveling & Porter is justly famed for its steam road rollers, with a basic design continuing in production for 50 years; while other manufacturers also made rollers, some in large numbers, it is the Aveling that the public recognises as the humble road-making steam engine that came down every road and street, until superseded by modern technology.

Thomas Aveling, a farmer interested in engineering, started an agricultural machinery repair shop in 1850 in Rochester, Kent. He experimented with traction engine and agricultural machinery design throughout the 1850s, and set up an iron foundry and engineering firm, also in Rochester. He also had workshops at Strood, Kent, where at a later date the famous Invicta Works was built. The emblem of Kent is the 'rampant' horse, and every engine from the factory carried this emblem together with the word 'Invicta' below, the Latin word for 'unconquered'. In 1862 Richard Porter brought capital and his name to the firm, which from then on became Aveling & Porter Ltd.

Besides the company's famous steam rollers, Aveling & Porter made ploughing engines, portables, agricultural traction engines, steam tractors, road locomotives and showman's engines, wagons, and a full range of agricultural equipment. However, it was the steam roller that dominated production, representing two-thirds of total output. The firm expanded during the later years of Queen Victoria's reign, and by 1895 was employing a thousand workers, and selling its products around the world, Australia being an important market.

After the First World War, as with many steam engineering companies, falling orders due to the march of the internal combustion engine compelled Aveling & Porter to join the Agricultural & General Engineers Ltd consortium, which failed in 1932. The road roller side of the business was bought by Barfords, and Aveling-Barford Ltd of Grantham continued to make steam rollers, and eventually internal-combustion-engined rollers, to recent times. There are 600 examples preserved in this country, of which 75% are steam rollers.

Silver Link Publishing Ltd
The Trundle
Ringstead Road
Great Addington
Kettering
Northants NN14 4BW

Tel/Fax: 01536 330588

email: sales@nostalgiacollection.com
Website: www.nostalgiacollection.com

Printed and bound in Česká Republika

Wagons and locomotives

TARRANT HINTON The 1922 A&P Class FGPA wagon *Lady Fiona*, imported from Australia, is seen at the Great Dorset Steam Fair in September 1994.

QUAINTON ROAD Traction engines on rail: two A&P rail locomotives at the Buckinghamshire Railway Centre in June 2001.

Below: **TARRANT HINTON** 1900 Class LC6 road locomotive *Jimmy* working hard at the Great Dorset Steam Fair in September 1999.

Above: **RUSHMOOR** The Rushmoor Rally no longer takes place, but back in July 1998 featured 1914 Class YLD road locomotive *Clyde*.

Traction Engines and Tractors

FROMEBRIDGE MILL Participating in a local club road run in Gloucestershire in September 2003 is 1899 Class AC6 traction engine *Queen Victoria*.

MUCH MARCLE At the Marcle Rally of July 2004 *Queen Victoria* is belted to a Foster threshing drum.

Right: **TARRANT HINTON** 1907 Class XAC4 tractor *Little Lucy* was photographed at the Great Dorset Steam Fair in August 2002 .

Below: **OLD WARDEN** 1907 Class XAC4 *Queen of Herts* is a CRR – Convertible Road Roller – and is seen at the National Traction Engine Trust Apprentices Weekend at Shuttleworth House in June 2003. Convertibles were engines that were delivered from the factory usually as a roller with the necessary equipment to be converted into a tractor, or vice versa.

UPTON ON SEVERN This rally was the forerunner of the Welland Rally, and in July 1993 one of the participants was 1914 Class BLD tractor *Mendip Star*.

KEMBLE Since 2011 this rally has taken place at South Cerney, but catching the last rays of the setting sun at Kemble in July 2004 is 1914 Class GND tractor *Princess Victoria*.

FAIRFORD This Gloucestershire rally is no longer held, but posing there in July 1998 is 1920 Class KLD traction engine *Jubilee*.

KNOWL HILL This Berkshire rally is another that no longer takes place. *Jubilee* is seen again there in August 2002.

OLD WARDEN Another 1920 A&P product, Class KND tractor *Clementine*, is seen at the Bedfordshire Steam Rally in September 2003.

Left: **LITTLE CHALFONT** 1920 Class KND tractor *Shamrock* is taking part in the Chilterns Road Run of October 2003.

Below: **NEAR STOWMARKET** 1923 Class A tractor *Old Peculiar* takes part in the East Suffolk Road Run in July 2003.

Below left: **BUXHALL** Another shot of *Old Peculiar* during the same event.

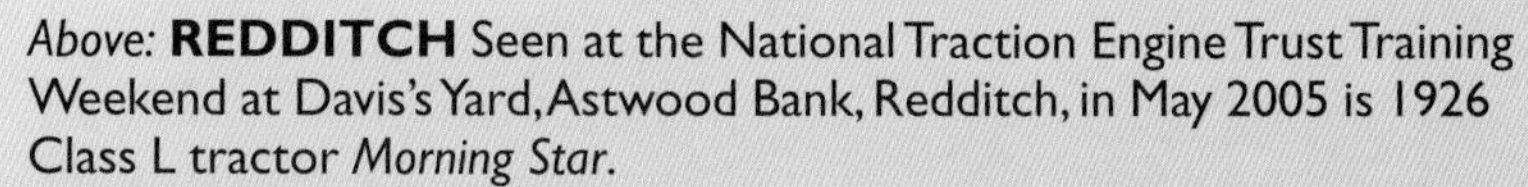

Above: **REDDITCH** Seen at the National Traction Engine Trust Training Weekend at Davis's Yard, Astwood Bank, Redditch, in May 2005 is 1926 Class L tractor *Morning Star*.

Top right: **ELVASTON** At this rally in July 2002 we see two A&P engines, *Morning Star* again on the right, and an 1884 Class A6, the third-oldest to have been preserved.

Right: **BUXHALL** 1926 Class M tractor *Nippy* during an East Suffolk Road Run.

WEETING On show at the July 1998 rally is 1926 Class XAC4 tractor *Julie*.

Inset left: **MUCH MARCLE** In the parade ring at the Marcle Rally in July 2004 is 1927 Class B Convertible tractor *Tolerance*.

Left: **BEAMISH** 1930 Class AD tractor *Hunslet* was photographed in May 2008.

Below: **TARRANT HINTON** 1931 Class L tractor *Orinoco* featured at the Great Dorset Steam Fair in August 2000.

Road rollers

BANBURY At the June 2003 rally 1894 A&P Class R10 10-ton road roller *Sarah* takes part in a recreation of road-making.

Left: **UPTON ON SEVERN** This 1901 Class R10 10-ton road roller, at the Upton on Severn Rally in July 1991, is without its later canopy.

Above: **CHIPPING NORTON** The same roller is seen in November 2000 on a local club road run at Walk Farm, Chipping Norton, with the canopy fitted.

Left: **ST AGNES** At this Cornwall Rally in August 1992 is 1904 Class XA3 5-ton road roller *Bo Peep*.

Above: **TALLINGTON** At this rally in May 1998 is 1904 Class R10 10-ton road roller *Lady of the Manor*. The rally is now held at Belvoir Castle.

WEETING 1907 Class R12 12-ton road roller *Big Bertha* is seen at the Weeting Rally in July 2002.

Above: **OLD WARDEN** Posed in front of Shuttleworth House during the Bedfordshire Steam Rally of September 2005 is a 1908 Class AM6 2RR 6-ton road roller.

Right: **GOVERS HILL** 1912 Class BS 10-ton road roller *Evening Star* negotiates a junction at Govers Hill, Cornwall, during the West of England Steam Engine Society Road Run in July 1995.

STOKE ROW En route to the Stoke Row Rally is 1914 Class QTD 8-ton road roller *Little Gem*.

Left: **KNOWL HILL** The August 1993 rally included 1915 Class BT 6-ton road roller *Albert Webb*.

Below: **MOIRA** This Leicestershire Steam Gala no longer takes place, but attending in September 1991 was 1915 Class BS 10-ton road roller *Monarch*.

Right: **TODDINGTON** Heading from Toddington to Stanway House is 1915 Class BS road roller *Britannia*. It is on the way to the Gloucestershire Warwickshire Railway Steam & Vintage Rally in October 2003, an event that no longer takes place.

HENRI COLLINGS GOVILON ABERGAVENNY
AF 4442

Left: **LITTLE CHALFONT** Entering Honors Yard, Little Chalfont, in October 2003 is 1916 Class BHP 15-ton road roller *Jupiter*.

Above: **RUSHMOOR** Photographed at the July 1998 rally is a 1916 Class BT 10-ton road roller.

INKBERROW With trailer in tow, 1920 Class BS 10-ton road roller *Major* is on a local club road run in this Worcestershire village.

L 8953

Opposite: **DUDLEY** By the weighbridge at the Black Country Living Museum in July 2007 is 1920 Class BSD 10-ton road roller *Sarah*.

Left: **EAST ANGLIA** Out in the country on an East Anglian Road Run is 1920 Class BS 10-ton road roller *Starchy*.

Above: **ECTON PARK** This rally no longer takes place, but attending in August 1994 is 1922 Class E 10-ton road roller *Gulliver*.

MUCH MARCLE Seen at the Marcle Rally of July 2006 is this 1922 Class D 8-ton road roller.

LONGPARISH On a local club run from Marders Yard, Oxdrove, 1922 Class C 8-ton road roller *Stoneybroke* passes through the Hampshire village.

ABERYSTWYTH Actual rolling is taking place at St Michael's Church, Aberystwyth, in June 1996. The engine is 8-ton 1922 Class GND *Lady Hesketh*.

GOVERS HILL During the West of England Steam Engine Society Road Run of May 1995, 1923 Class C 8-ton road roller *Little Peter* is seen at Govers Hill, Cornwall.

SUTTON BASSETT On a local Leicestershire club run in June 2003 is this 1923 Class E 10-ton road roller.

CASTLE COMBE At the Castle Combe Rally in September 1993 is 1923 Class E 10-ton road roller *Hercules*.

MOIRA 1923 Class F 10-ton road roller *Katie* poses at the September 1991 Steam Gala.

STOKE ROW In action at the June 2000 rally, 1923 Class E 10-ton road roller *Churchill* is rolling a footpath.

HANBURY 1923 Class F 10-ton road roller *Lord Malvern* participates in a local club road run in September 2002.

BANBURY On the field at the June 1992 rally is 1924 Class E 10-ton road roller *Phoenix*.

BEAMISH Two portraits of 1924 Class C 8-ton road roller *Julia*, taken in May 2008.

BROMSGROVE At Avoncroft, Bromsgrove, in April 1992 is 1924 Class G 12-ton road roller *Penare*.

BEAMISH Also photographed at Beamish in May 2008 is 1925 Class D 8-ton road roller *Ayesha*.

INKBERROW 1925 Class A 6-ton road roller *Acrise Maid* pauses to take on water during a local club road run in May 1990.

Left: **LEDBURY** Climbing towards Ledbury on a road run in August 1994 is 1926 Class C 8-ton road roller *Viatect*.

Above: **BRIXWORTH** Also climbing, this time during the National Traction Engine Trust 50th Road Run in September 1996, is 1928 Class E 10-ton road roller *Evelyn* near Brixworth, Northamptonshire.

ALCESTER HEATH 1932 Class AB 8-ton road roller *Daisy* is on a local club road run in September 1992.

Left: **KEMBLE** At the former Kemble Rally in August 2003 is this 1934 Class AD 10-ton road roller.

Above: **RUSHMOOR** Photographed at the Rushmoor Rally in May 1998 is 1911 Class MLD 2RR 6-ton road roller *Chimaera*, a roller experimentally using the Shay principle (used on some logging railways). Not particularly successful, this is the only survivor.

Below: **WELFORD ON AVON** Another Aveling-Barford roller, this time the 1937 Class W 10-ton *Patricia*.

Above: **NEAR SHIPSTON ON STOUR** Climbing a Warwickshire lane is a 1938 Class R Aveling-Barford 6-ton road roller. The firm of Barfords took over the rolling manufacture from Aveling & Porter, having been part of the amalgamation of steam companies like Burrell and Garrett known as Agricultural & General Engineers Ltd in the 1920s.

STORRINGTON 1937 Aveling-Barford Class W 10-ton road roller *Prince of Wales* at Storrington Rally in June 1992.

STOKE ROW Roading into the Stoke Row Rally in June 1996 is another 1937 Class W 10-ton road roller.

Index